"9Marks, as a ministry, has taken basic biblical teaching about the church and put it into the hands of pastors. Bobby, by way of these study guides, has taken this teaching and delivered it to the person in the pew. I am unaware of any other tool that so thoroughly and practically helps Christians understand God's plan for the local church. I can't wait to use these studies in my own congregation."

Jeramie Rinne, Senior Pastor, South Shore Baptist Church, Hingham, Massachusetts

"Bobby Jamieson has done local church pastors an incredible service by writing these study guides. Clear, biblical, and practical, they introduce the biblical basis for a healthy church. But more importantly, they challenge and equip church members to be part of the process of improving their own church's health. The studies work for individual, small group, and larger group settings. I have used them for the last year at my own church and appreciate how easy they are to adapt to my own setting. I don't know of anything else like them. Highly recommended!"

Michael Lawrence, Senior Pastor, Hinson Baptist Church, *Biblical Theology in the Life of the Church*

"This is a Bible study that is actually rooted in the Bible and involves actual study. In the 9Marks Healthy Church Study Guides series a new standard has been set for personal theological discovery and corresponding personal application. Rich exposition, compelling questions, and clear syntheses combine to give a guided tour of ecclesiology—the theology of the church. I know of no better curriculum for generating understanding of and involvement in the church than this. It will be a welcome resource in our church for years to come."

Rick Holland, Senior Pastor, Mission Road Bible Church, Prairie Village, Kansas

"In America today we have the largest churches in the history of our nation, but the least amount of impact for Christ's kingdom. Slick marketing and finely polished vision statements are a foundation of sand. The 9Marks Healthy Church Study Guides series is a refreshing departure from church-growth materials, towards an in-depth study of God's Word that will equip God's people with his vision for his Church. These study guides will lead local congregations to abandon secular methodologies for church growth and instead rely on Christ's principles for developing healthy, God-honoring assemblies."

Carl J. Broggi, Senior Pastor, Community Bible Church, Beaufort, South Carolina; President, Search the Scriptures Radio Ministry

"Anyone who loves Jesus will love what Jesus loves. The Bible clearly teaches that Jesus loves the church. He knows about and cares for individual churches and wants them to be spiritually healthy and vibrant. Not only has Jesus laid down his life for the church but he has also given many instructions in his Word regarding how churches are to live and function in the world. This series of Bible studies by 9Marks shows how Scripture teaches these things. Any Christian who works through this curriculum, preferably with other believers, will be helped to see in fresh ways the wisdom, love, and power of God in establishing the church on earth. These studies are biblical, practical, and accessible. I highly recommend this curriculum as a useful tool that will help any church embrace its calling to display the glory of God to a watching world."

Thomas Ascol, Senior Pastor, Grace Baptist Church of Cape Coral, Florida; Executive Director, Founders Ministries

9MARKS HEALTHY CHURCH STUDY GUIDES

Built upon the Rock: The Church

Hearing God's Word: Expositional Preaching

The Whole Truth about God: Biblical Theology

God's Good News: The Gospel

Real Change: Conversion

Reaching the Lost: Evangelism

Committing to One Another: Church Membership

Guarding One Another: Church Discipline

Growing One Another: Discipleship in the Church

Leading One Another: Church Leadership

BUILT UPON
THE ROCK:
THE CHURCH

Bobby Jamieson

Mark Dever, General Editor

Jonathan Leeman, Managing Editor

HEALTHY CHURCH STUDY GUIDES

CROSSWAY

WHEATON, ILLINOIS

Built upon the Rock: The Church

Copyright © 2012 by 9Marks

Published by Crossway
    1300 Crescent Street
    Wheaton, Illinois 60187

Cover design: Dual Identity inc.

First printing 2012

Printed in the United States of America

Unless otherwise indicated, Scripture quotations are from the ESV® Bible (*The Holy Bible, English Standard Version®*), copyright © 2001 by Crossway. Used by permission. All rights reserved.

Scripture references marked NIV are taken from *The Holy Bible, New International Version®*, NIV®. Copyright © 1973, 1978, 1984, 2011 by Biblica, Inc.™ Used by permission. All rights reserved worldwide.

All emphases in Scripture have been added by the author.

Trade paperback ISBN: 978-1-4335-2524-7

PDF ISBN: 978-1-4335-2525-4

Mobipocket ISBN: 978-1-4335-2526-1

ePub ISBN: 978-1-4335-2527-8

Crossway is a publishing ministry of Good News Publishers.

LB		20	19	18	17	16	15	14	13	12
15	14	13	12	11	10	9	8	7	6	5	4	3	2	1

CONTENTS

INTRODUCTION

What does the local church mean to you?

Maybe you love your church. You love the people. You love the preaching and the singing. You can't wait to show up on Sunday, and you cherish fellowship with other church members throughout the week.

Then again, maybe your church is just a place you show up to a couple times a month. You sneak in late, duck out early.

We at 9Marks are convinced that the local church is where God means to display his glory to the nations. And we want to help you catch this vision, together with your whole church.

The 9Marks Healthy Church Study Guides are a series of six- or seven-week studies on each of the "nine marks of a healthy church" plus one introductory study. These nine marks are the core convictions of our ministry. To provide a quick introduction to them, we've included a chapter from Mark Dever's book *What Is a Healthy Church?* with each study. We don't claim that these nine marks are the most important things about the church or the only important things about the church. But we do believe that they are biblical and therefore helpful for churches.

So, in these studies, we're going to work through the biblical foundations and practical applications of each mark. The ten studies are:

- *Built upon the Rock: The Church* (the introductory study)
- *Hearing God's Word: Expositional Preaching*
- *The Whole Truth about God: Biblical Theology*
- *God's Good News: The Gospel*
- *Real Change: Conversion*
- *Reaching the Lost: Evangelism*
- *Committing to One Another: Church Membership*

- *Guarding One Another: Church Discipline*
- *Growing One Another: Discipleship in the Church*
- *Leading One Another: Church Leadership*

Each session of these studies takes a close look at one or more passages of Scripture and considers how to apply it to the life of your congregation. We hope they are equally appropriate for Sunday schools, small groups, and other contexts where a group of two to two-hundred people can gather to discuss God's Word.

These studies are mainly driven by observation, interpretation, and application questions—so get ready to speak up! We also hope that these studies provide opportunities for people to reflect together on their experiences in the church, whatever those experiences may be.

The study you are now holding is called *Built upon the Rock* because Jesus promised to build his church upon the "rock" of people like Peter when they confess that he is the Messiah. Not only that, Jesus promised that the church would prevail against the gates of hell (Matt. 16:16–18). Clearly the church matters to Jesus, and it should matter to us, too!

That's why this study works through seven biblical aspects of the church. By looking at these seven biblical concepts, we're going to discover a big-picture vision of the church. What is the church? Why did Jesus establish a church? How does the church fit into God's plans in Scripture? What's the big deal about church anyway? Does it matter whether I'm a member? What should life in the church be like?

Are you ready?

WHAT A CHURCH IS . . . AND ISN'T

BY MARK DEVER

(Adapted from chapter 1 of What Is a Healthy Church?*)*

What is a church? That's a tough question. And Christians today are looking for all sorts of different things in their churches.

A JARRING CONVERSATION

During my graduate studies, I remember one conversation with a friend who worked for a Christian ministry that was not affiliated with any one church. He and I did attend the same church for a couple of years. But while I joined the church as a member, my friend didn't. In fact, he only came for the Sunday morning service and would slip in about halfway through, just in time for the sermon.

One day, I decided to ask him about his halfhearted attendance. "I don't really get anything out of the rest of the service," he replied.

"Have you ever thought of joining the church?" I asked.

He appeared genuinely surprised by my question and responded, "Join the church? I honestly don't know why I would do that. I know what I'm here for, and those people would just slow me down."

As far as I could tell, he didn't say those words disdainfully, but with the genuine zeal of a gifted evangelist who did not want to waste one hour of the Lord's time. He had given some thought to what he was looking for in a church. And on the whole it didn't involve the other members of the church, at least not that church. He wanted a place where he could hear good preaching from God's Word and get his spiritual jolt for the week.

Yet his words reverberated in my mind—"those people would just slow me down." There were a number of things I wanted to say, but all I said was, "But did you ever think that if you linked arms with those people, yes, they may slow you down, but you may help to speed them up? Have you thought that might be a part of God's plan for them, and for you?"

I, too, wanted a church where I could hear good preaching every Sunday. But the words "body of Christ" mean more than just that, don't they?

A PEOPLE, NOT A PLACE

The church is not a place. It's not a building. It's not a preaching point. It's not a spiritual service provider. It's a people—the new covenant, blood-bought people of God. That's why Paul said, "Christ loved the church and gave himself up for her" (Eph. 5:25 NIV). He didn't give himself up for a place but for a people.

That's why the church I pastor starts its Sunday morning gatherings not by saying, "Welcome to Capitol Hill Baptist Church," but, "Welcome to this gathering of the Capitol Hill Baptist Church." We are a people who gather. Yes, this is a small thing, but we're trying to point to a big reality even in the words we use to welcome people.

Remembering that the church is a people should help us recognize what's important and what's not important. I know I need the help. For example, I have a temptation to let something like the style of music dictate how I feel about a church. After all, the style of music a church uses is one of the first things we will notice about any church, and we tend to respond to music at a very emotional level. Music makes us feel a certain way. Yet what does it say about my love for Christ and for Christ's people if I decide to leave a church because of the style of its music? Or if, when pastoring a church, I marginalize a majority of my congregation because I think the style of music needs to be updated? At the very least, we could say that I've forgotten that the church, fundamentally, is a people and not a place.

At the same time, the Bible teaches that Christians should very much care about what happens at a church—what it does. In fact, the latter half of this book is devoted to such a discussion.

How do we balance these two things—caring about a people but also caring about what they do? If this were a book about raising Christian families, we would talk about doing certain things: eating dinner together, reading Scripture together, laughing together, praying for one another, and so on. Yet throughout the discussion, hopefully we would all remember that parents make mistakes and that kids will be kids. The family is not just an institution; it's a group of people.

So it is with a church. Does a particular church fail to meet your expectations in terms of what it does, as in whether it follows what the Bible says about church leadership (one topic that I'll cover later)? If so, remember that this is a group of people who are still growing in grace. Love them. Serve them. Be patient with them. Again, think of a family. Whenever your parents, siblings, or children fail to meet your expectations, do you suddenly throw them out of the family? I hope you forgive and are patient with them. You might even stop to consider whether it's your expectations that should be adjusted! By this same token, we should ask ourselves whether we know how to love and persevere with church members who have different opinions, who fail to meet expectations, or even who sin against us. (Don't you and I have sin that ever needs to be forgiven?)

Somewhere, of course, there is a line. There are some churches you may not want to join, or pastor, or remain joined to. We'll return to this question in the section on the essential marks of a church. For the time being, the basic principle remains the same: the church is a people. And whatever we're looking for, or whatever we're saying the church should be, must be guided by that basic, biblical principle.

A PEOPLE, NOT A STATISTIC

Let me put up one more road block to bad thinking about the church, thinking especially common among pastors. Not only is the church not a place, but it's also not a statistic.

When I was in graduate school, I remember encountering a letter of counsel written by John Brown, a pastor in the nineteenth century, to one of his students who had just been ordained over a small congregation. In the letter Brown wrote:

> I know the vanity of your heart, and that you will feel mortified that your congregation is very small, in comparison with those of your brethren around you; but assure yourself on the word of an old man, that when you come to give an account of them to the Lord Christ, at his judgment-seat, you will think you have had enough.[1]

As I considered the congregation over which God had given me charge, I felt the weightiness of this day of accounting before God. Did I want the church I pastored to become big? Popular and much discussed? A church that in some way looked impressive?

Was I motivated in any way to just "put up with" or "tolerate" the group of people in front of me, to bide my time and wait for opportunities to make the church into what I thought it should be? Not that having desires for a church's future is bad, but were my desires leading me to be indifferent, even annoyed, with the saints surrounding me in the present?

Or would I remember what was infinitely at stake for the several scores of souls, most of them elderly, already sitting in front of me on Sunday mornings in a room big enough for eight hundred? Would I love and serve these few, even if their unbiblical committees, and old-fashioned traditions, and not-my-favorite music selections stood in the way of my (I think legitimate) hopes for the church? And I know it's not only pastors who fall into "tolerating" the people around them, biding their time until the church becomes what they envision it can be.

The church is a people, not a place or a statistic. It's a body united into him who is the head. It's a family joined together by adoption through Christ.

I pray that we pastors would increasingly recognize our awesome responsibility for the particular flocks over which God has made us undershepherds.

---

[1] James Hay and Henry Belfrage, *Memoir of the Rev. Alexander Waugh* (Edinburgh: William Oliphant and Son, 1839), 64–65.

But I also pray that you, Christian, whether an elder or an infant in the faith, would increasingly recognize your responsibility to love, serve, encourage, and hold accountable the rest of your church family. When it comes to your flesh-and-blood siblings, I trust that you already recognize where Cain went wrong when he dismissively said to the Lord, "Am I my brother's keeper?" But even more I hope that you recognize, if you haven't already, your higher responsibility to the brothers and sisters of your church family.

> A crowd was sitting around [Jesus], and they told him, "Your mother and brothers are outside looking for you."
> "Who are my mother and my brothers?" he asked.
> Then he looked at those seated in a circle around him and said, "Here are my mother and my brothers! Whoever does God's will is my brother and sister and mother." (Mark 3:32–35 NIV)

WEEK 1
THE PEOPLE OF GOD

GETTING STARTED

Alyssa is a thirty-two-year-old single woman who is a member of your church. By all appearances, Alyssa would make a great wife and mother, and she deeply desires to get married and start a family. Mr. Right hasn't come along yet, but she keeps hoping.

One day, you find out that she is seeing someone. When you ask her about it, the conversation reveals that he is not a believer. She knows the Bible speaks against this, but she's tired of waiting. Things are getting pretty serious, and they are even talking about marriage.

1. What do you do when you find out about Alyssa's relationship?

2. Do you think that the church should do anything about this? Is it the business of members to stick their noses in people's private lives?

Independence and Autonomy

In the modern West, we like to think that we don't depend on anyone else and that we can do whatever we want. We like to think of ourselves as both independent and autonomous.

Do you see how these two things go together? We like to be free from entangling commitments to others (independent) so that we are free to do what we want (autonomous, literally, "a law unto oneself"). Think of how American culture glorifies the rugged individualist or the self-made millionaire who grows so powerful that he gets to make his own rules.

So most people would say of Alyssa's relationship, "What she does with her life is her business, and the church should stay out of it." But as we're going to see from Scripture, God's claim on our lives demands much more.

MAIN IDEA

Through Jesus Christ, God is saving not only individuals but also *a people*. The church is the people of God. This means that, as Christians, we are neither independent nor autonomous. Rather, we belong to God and to the people of God. So we are to submit to God's will and to one another.

DIGGING IN

In Ephesians 2:11–16, Paul speaks about how our salvation as individuals incorporates us into God's one redeemed people. Then, in Ephesians 2:17–22, Paul writes:

> [17] And he came and preached peace to you who were far off and peace to those who were near. [18] For through him we both have access in one Spirit to the Father. [19] So then you are no longer strangers and aliens, but you are fellow citizens with the saints and members of the household of God, [20] built on the foundation of the apostles and prophets, Christ Jesus himself being the cornerstone, [21] in whom the whole structure, being joined together, grows into a holy temple in the Lord. [22] In him you also are being built together into a dwelling place for God by the Spirit.

1. What phrases does Paul use in verses 17 and 19 to describe what we were as non-Christians? What do those phrases mean?

2. In verse 19, what two phrases does Paul use to describe our new state as Christians? What does this teach us about what happens to us when we become Christians?

3. Given our new identity which Paul describes in verses 19 through 22, should we Christians view ourselves as autonomous, independent individuals? Explain.

In 2 Corinthians 6:14–18 we read,

> [14] Do not be unequally yoked with unbelievers. For what partnership has righteousness with lawlessness? Or what fellowship has light

with darkness? ¹⁵ What accord has Christ with Belial? Or what portion does a believer share with an unbeliever? ¹⁶ What agreement has the temple of God with idols? For we are the temple of the living God; as God said,

> "I will make my dwelling among them and walk among them,
>   and I will be their God,
>   and they shall be my people.
> ¹⁷ Therefore go out from their midst,
>   and be separate from them, says the Lord,
> and touch no unclean thing;
>   then I will welcome you,
> ¹⁸ and I will be a father to you,
>   and you shall be sons and daughters to me,
> says the Lord Almighty."

4. List the different terms and images that Paul (quoting Leviticus 26:12 and Isaiah 52:11) uses to describe the church in relation to God:

5. In verse 16 God says of Christians, "I will be their God, and they shall be my people." Christians are possessed by God. What obligations do the people of God have because of this special relationship to God? (Hint: Notice the "therefore" in v. 17.)

6. Whose character are the people of God to represent? What does this say about our desire to be autonomous?

7. Have you ever thought about how becoming a Christian means becoming part of a new people, the people of God? In light of the two passages we've discussed, how should this truth change?

    a) Your relationship to other Christians?
    b) Your relationship to non-Christians?

8. If we better grasped this idea of being "a people," how would that affect our interactions in the local church?

9. Once we grasp the fact that, as a church, we are the people of God, both an encouragement and a challenge follow. The encouragement comes from knowing that we're God's treasured possession, the people he has specially loved and called to himself (Ex. 19:5; Rom. 1:6; 1 Pet. 2:9). This is not because of any goodness in us, but because of his sheer grace (Deut. 7:7–8; 2 Tim. 1:9). Further, it means that God is committed to being our God. He will be with us in the present and will one day bring us to live in perfect, face-to-face fellowship with himself (Matt. 28:20; Heb. 13:5; Rev. 21:3–4; 22:4).

On the other hand, the challenge of being the people of God comes from the fact that God calls us to submit, to obey, and to reflect his character to the world. What are some specific ways that being part of the people of God encourages you? Challenges you?

10. Think back to Alyssa from the beginning of the story. In view of the Bible's teaching that we as Christians are the people of God,

- How would you personally counsel Alyssa about her relationship?
- What should the church do about Alyssa's relationship?

WEEK 2
THE BODY OF CHRIST

GETTING STARTED

1. Imagine that you are moving to another city, and you don't know any Christians there. Your first order of business is to find a church. List five to ten things that you would look for in a church.

Many of us tend to treat the church as we treat most other things in life: as consumers. We want to receive certain goods and services that fulfill our desires (which we sometimes call "needs"). And we want to obtain these goods and services at a good price.

Since we act as consumers in so many areas of life, it seems only natural to do the same in church. But as we'll see in the following study, Scripture teaches that our attitude toward church should be just the opposite.

2. What are some ways that Christianity challenges consumerism?

MAIN IDEA

Scripture teaches that Christians should not approach the church as consumers but as members of a body. This means that we are to commit to one another, depend on one another, honor one another, and care for one another. In all we do in the church, we should seek not the fulfillment of our own desires but the common good.

DIGGING IN

In 1 Corinthians 12 Paul begins discussing spiritual gifts, which the Corinthians had been using in self-serving ways. In the opening verses of the chapter, Paul reminds them that all their different gifts are given by the same Spirit and for the common good. Then in verses 12–26 Paul writes,

> [12] For just as the body is one and has many members, and all the members of the body, though many, are one body, so it is with Christ. [13] For in one Spirit we were all baptized into one body—Jews or Greeks, slaves or free—and all were made to drink of one Spirit.
>
> [14] For the body does not consist of one member but of many. [15] If the foot should say, "Because I am not a hand, I do not belong to the body," that would not make it any less a part of the body. [16] And if the ear should say, "Because I am not an eye, I do not belong to the body," that would not make it any less a part of the body. [17] If the whole body were an eye, where would be the sense of hearing? If the whole body were an ear, where would be the sense of smell? [18] But as it is, God arranged the members in the body, each one of them, as he chose. [19] If all were a single member, where would the body be? [20] As it is, there are many parts, yet one body.
>
> [21] The eye cannot say to the hand, "I have no need of you," nor again the head to the feet, "I have no need of you." [22] On the contrary, the parts of the body that seem to be weaker are indispensable, [23] and on those parts of the body that we think less honorable we bestow the greater honor, and our unpresentable parts are treated with greater modesty, [24] which our more presentable parts do not require. But God has so composed the body, giving greater honor to the part that lacked it, [25] that there may be no division in the body, but that the members may have the same care for one another. [26] If one member suffers, all suffer together; if one member is honored, all rejoice together.

When Paul writes in verse 13 that we were all baptized into one body, he teaches that all of us are united to Christ and to one another. This profound unity we have with Christ, in other words, is also the foundation of our unity with one another.

While Paul's language in verses 12 and 13 refers most naturally to the universal church (that is, the total number of God's people throughout history), the rest of the passage clearly refers to concrete relationships in the local church. This makes perfect sense because, according to the whole New Testament, local church membership is how we "put on" and testify to our membership in the universal church.

For instance, think of how the New Testament describes the relationship between the righteous standing we have in Christ and our need to "put on" righteous actions. We *are* righteous in Christ, and we prove that by striving to live righteous lives (see especially Rom. 6:1–14; Col. 3:9–10).

Our church membership is similar. As Christians, we *are* members of Christ's universal church, and we "put on" that membership through membership in a local church. Thus, one implication of this passage of Scripture is that all Christians should, by definition, be members of local churches.

1. What is the overarching metaphor Paul uses to describe the church throughout this passage?

2. What do the "foot" and the "ear" say in verses 15 and 16? What attitude or emotion does this express?

3. In verses 17 to 20, Paul essentially makes two points for the "foot" and the "ear." What are they?

4. Read verses 19–20. If you are tempted to think like the "foot" and the "ear," how do these verses encourage you?

5. What do the "eye" and the "head" say in verse 21? What attitude does this express?

6. What are the two main points in Paul's response to the "eye" and the "head" (vv. 22–25)?

7. What does Paul say about the parts of the body that seem to be weaker (v. 22)? In light of this, how we should treat church members who do not seem impressive to us?

8. According to verse 25, God seems to have two goals for arranging the parts as he does. What are they? What is the example he gives in verse 26 to illustrate these things?

9. In light of this passage, how is a "Lone-Ranger Christian," who tries to live out his or her discipleship to Christ independently of others, misguided?

10. Back in verse 7, Paul articulates a priority that he returns to over and over. He writes, "To each is given the manifestation of the Spirit for the common good." *In 14:12 he says, "Since you are eager for manifestations of the Spirit,* strive to excel in building up the church." *And again in 14:26 he says, "Let all things be done for* building up."

This is the exact opposite of a consumer mentality. Consumers seek to fulfill their desires. Christians on the other hand are called to build up others and to seek the common good.

What are some practical ways that we can reject consumerism and seek the common good in how we relate to:

a) The church's corporate gatherings?
b) Listening to sermons?
c) Older members of the church?
d) Young mothers?
e) Widows?
f) Singles?

If you need a head start in thinking about specifics, consider that, according to Paul, we are to honor (vv. 23–24), care for (v. 25), suffer with (v. 26), and rejoice with (v. 26) other members of the body.

11. Go back to the list of things you made at the beginning of this study of what you would look for in a church. Is there anything you'd change?

WEEK 3
THE TEMPLE OF THE SPIRIT

GETTING STARTED

People give all kinds of reasons not to join a church:

- "The church just wants my money."
- "I'm too busy to be a member of a church."
- "Why should I join the church when I don't know if I'll still be living here in five or ten years?"
- "Membership is just a needless formality. What matters is that I'm serving in the church."

1. What are some other reasons you've heard people give for not joining a church or maybe have given yourself?

2. What difference do you think it makes whether a Christian is a member of a church?

MAIN IDEA

The church is the temple of the Holy Spirit—a joined-together, growing, holy dwelling place for God. Therefore, every Christian should be a member of a church and should seek the unity, holiness, and growth of the church.

DIGGING IN

In Ephesians 2, Paul joyfully proclaims the riches of God's saving grace in Christ. In the first ten verses Paul teaches that we are individually saved by God's grace through faith in Christ, not by works. In the rest of the chapter, Paul explains that through Christ, Gentiles and Jews now constitute one new people.

In Ephesians 2:19–22, Paul elaborates on this new unity that Jews and Gentiles have in Christ:

> [19] So then you are no longer strangers and aliens, but you are fellow citizens with the saints and members of the household of God,[20] built on the foundation of the apostles and prophets, Christ Jesus himself being the cornerstone, [21] in whom the whole structure, being joined together, grows into a holy temple in the Lord.[22] In him you also are being built together into a dwelling place for God by the Spirit.

1. List the different images and metaphors in these verses that Paul uses to describe the unity that Jews and Gentiles have in Christ (some of them overlap):

In this study we are going to focus entirely on the last metaphor Paul uses—the church is the temple, the dwelling place, of God.

Under the old covenant, the temple was the place where God made his presence felt. It was the place that God publicly identified himself with. And it was the place where people came to worship and offer sacrifices that maintained their relationships with God.

Now, through Christ's death and resurrection, Christ himself has become the temple. He is the "place" where God's wrath was propitiated and where people are reconciled to God (see John 2:19–21). Not only that, everyone who is united to Christ by faith becomes God's temple. God's Holy Spirit dwells within us and God publicly identifies himself with his church.

2. What is the "foundation" Paul describes in verse 20? Why is this foundation essential for the life and health of the church?

3. In verse 21 Paul describes the whole of God's people when he says that "the whole structure, being joined together, grows into a holy temple in the Lord." This means that now, the entire people of God are the dwelling place of God, which he will perfectly and permanently indwell one day (see Rev. 21:3–4; 21:22).

Yet in verse 22 Paul says "you also"—meaning the church in Ephesus—"are being built together into a dwelling place for God by the Spirit." This means that the local church is a joined-together, built-together temple of God. All its members are joined together, interlocking with one another and with Christ the cornerstone (v. 20).

Do you think that a Christian is living in line with this reality if he or she is not a member of a local church? Why or why not?

4. If you were talking to a Christian who thought that he or she didn't need to join a church, how could you use this passage to encourage this person to become a member of a sound, gospel-preaching church?

5. When Paul writes that the church is being "built together into a dwelling place for God by the Spirit" (Eph. 2:22), he is likely referring to both numerical and spiritual growth. People are becoming Christians, and everyone is growing in holiness and maturity.

By what means does this growth take place? (Feel free to consult other New Testament passages such as Acts 2:41 and Ephesians 4:15–16.)

6. According to verse 22, who builds the temple that is the church?

7. In whom does he build it?

8. For whom does he build it?

9. Why should these last three points encourage Christians?

10. In 1 Corinthians 3:16–17 Paul writes, "Do you not know that you are God's temple and that God's Spirit dwells in you? If anyone destroys God's temple, God will destroy him. For God's temple is holy, and you are that temple."

And again in Ephesians 2:21 Paul writes that the church is growing "into a holy temple in the Lord."

The church is a holy temple, because God possesses it and because the Holy Spirit dwells in its members. How should the church's identity as God's holy temple impact:

    a) How a church goes about receiving new members?

    b) Whether a church should seek to actively oversee the lives of its members?

    c) How a church should respond to a member who refuses to repent of sin?

11. Because the church is growing into *a holy temple, the church is also called to grow in holiness (v. 21). How should this mandate for holiness impact:*

    a) The things we discuss when we meet with other church members?

    b) How we listen to sermons?

    c) What we look for in the church's corporate gatherings?

    d) What we desire to get out of the church's corporate gatherings?

    e) How we respond when others sin against us?

WEEK 4
THE LIVING CHURCH

GETTING STARTED

1. Have you ever been in a church where it seemed unusual for someone to be a growing Christian?

In some churches, there seems to be little expectation that people will actually grow in the knowledge of Christ, in obeying him, and in sharing the gospel with others. Instead, members' lives are on spiritual autopilot. Christianity is a social label rather than an active, vibrant faith.

Sadly, churches like this are all too common. But this kind of nominal, stagnant religion should *not* characterize a church. The New Testament presents the opposite picture.

MAIN IDEA

The church is a living organism composed of spiritually alive, growing Christians. Therefore, the members of local churches should expect, encourage, and equip other members to grow spiritually.

DIGGING IN

In order to understand the church's nature as a living, Spirit-filled organism, we need to understand the history of God's dealings with his people.

When God called Israel out of slavery in Egypt, he gave them his law. Yet for centuries, Israel disobeyed God's law by turning their backs on him and serving false gods. Eventually, God punished them by kicking them out of the land he had given them.

But in Jeremiah 31:31–34 God says,

[31] Behold, the days are coming, declares the LORD, when I will make a new covenant with the house of Israel and the house of Judah, [32] not like the covenant that I made with their fathers on the day when I took them by the hand to bring them out of the land of Egypt, my covenant that they broke, though I was their husband, declares the LORD. [33] For this is the covenant that I will make with the house of Israel after those days, declares the LORD: I will put my law within them, and I will write it on their hearts. And I will be their God, and they shall be my people. [34] And no longer shall each one teach his neighbor and each his brother, saying, "Know the LORD," for they shall all know me, from the least of them to the greatest, declares the LORD. For I will forgive their iniquity, and I will remember their sin no more.

1. List the ways that this new covenant differs from the old one.

2. In Luke 22:20, Jesus explains that his sacrificial death brings this new covenant which Jeremiah spoke about into effect. The church, then, is the people of the new covenant. We are united to Christ by faith, we have our sins forgiven, we know the Lord, and we have God's law written on our hearts so that we can obey it by the power of God's Spirit.

    a) Given the realities of the new covenant, what's wrong with saying that someone can be a Christian and never grow spiritually?
    b) Does this mean that every day of our Christian lives will be marked by dramatic and bold growth? Explain.

The New Testament passages on church discipline teach us to expect that not everyone who professes the name of Christ in the church is necessarily a Christian. At the same time, we see throughout the New Testament that the church is a living, growing body:

- In 1 Peter 2:5, Peter writes that "you yourselves like living stones are being built up as a spiritual house, to be a holy priesthood, to offer spiritual sacrifices acceptable to God through Jesus Christ."
- In Ephesians 4:16 Paul writes that "the whole body, joined and held together by every joint with which it is equipped, when each part is working properly, makes the body grow so that it builds itself up in love."

3. In these two passages, what expectation do Peter and Paul place on every member?

4. Do you notice anything else about the nature of this growth? Does it occur in isolation from other Christians?

We've seen that God's new covenant creates a church composed of genuine, growing Christians. Now, we're going to spend the rest of this study focusing on the picture of one living, growing church that Paul gives us in 1 Thessalonians 1:2–10:

> [2] We give thanks to God always for all of you, constantly mentioning you in our prayers, [3] remembering before our God and Father your work of faith and labor of love and steadfastness of hope in our Lord Jesus Christ. [4] For we know, brothers loved by God, that he has chosen you, [5] because our gospel came to you not only in word, but also in power and in the Holy Spirit and with full conviction. You know what kind of men we proved to be among you for your sake. [6] And you became imitators of us and of the Lord, for you received the word in much affliction, with the joy of the Holy Spirit, [7] so that you became an example to all the believers in Macedonia and in Achaia. [8] For not only has the word of the Lord sounded forth from you in Macedonia and Achaia, but your faith in God has gone forth everywhere, so that we need not say anything. [9] For they themselves report concerning us the kind of reception we had among you, and how you turned to God from idols to serve the living and true God, [10] and to wait for his Son from heaven, whom he raised from the dead, Jesus who delivers us from the wrath to come.

5. How did the Thessalonians respond when Paul preached the gospel to them (vv. 6, 9)?

6. Can you summarize the difference between a genuine Christian who hears the message of the gospel and the nominal Christian who hears it? (A nominal Christian is a Christian in name only.)

7. To whose power does Paul attribute their response to the gospel (vv. 5–6)? Why does this leave no room for boasting?

8. Paul observes that the Thessalonians' received the gospel "in much affliction." How does this testify to the genuineness of their faith (v. 6)?

9. What does the Thessalonians' faith in Christ prompt them to do (vv. 3, 8–10)?

10. Suppose, looking at your own profession of faith, it looks like a nominal Christian's. There's a lack of conviction, a lack of joy, and a lack of turning from idols. What should you do?

We've seen in Jeremiah 31, Ephesians 4, and 1 Thessalonians 1 that Scripture teaches that churches are to be living bodies, filled with genuine, growing Christians. In view of this, we as church members should expect other church members to grow spiritually and should encourage them in that growth.

11. How should the expectation that members are growing spiritually shape:

- The purpose of small group meetings?
- What you do on Saturday nights in preparation for Sunday?
- How the church's elders or other leaders shepherd the church?
- Conversations after church?
- What the church's life looks like throughout the week? How do these lessons about corporate growth together translate into the rest of the week?

12. What are some ways you can encourage spiritual growth in church members who are:

- Struggling financially?
- Busy and under pressure at work?
- Overwhelmed at home with young children?
- Physically ill?
- Dealing with the death of a loved one, such as a spouse or child?
- Gifted in their knowledge of and ability to teach the Bible?

WEEK 5
THE GROWING CHURCH

GETTING STARTED

1. Have you ever known (or been!) a self-confessed Lone-Ranger Christian? (A Lone-Ranger Christian is someone who believes that growing as a Christian is a private matter between that person and God.)

MAIN IDEA

Christians grow as we buildup and are built up by other members of the body of Christ. According to Scripture, the way we attain Christian maturity is through the church.

DIGGING IN

In Ephesians 4, the apostle Paul turns from proclaiming the riches of what God has done for us in Christ to exhorting the Ephesian Christians to walk in a manner worthy of their calling (v. 1).

In the first six verses Paul exhorts the Ephesians to pursue unity in the church, and then in verses 7 through 10 he begins to explain how Christ has given gifts to his church. In verses 11 through 16 Paul continues,

> [11] And he gave the apostles, the prophets, the evangelists, the shepherds and teachers, [12] to equip the saints for the work of ministry, for building up the body of Christ, [13] until we all attain to the unity of the faith and of the knowledge of the Son of God, to mature manhood, to the measure of the stature of the fullness of Christ, [14] so that we may no longer be children, tossed to and fro by the waves and carried about by every wind of doctrine, by human cunning, by craftiness in deceitful schemes. [15] Rather, speaking the truth in love, we are to grow up in every way into him who is the head, into Christ, [16] from whom the whole body, joined and held together by every joint with

which it is equipped, when each part is working properly, makes the
body grow so that it builds itself up in love.

1. Why did Christ give apostles, prophets, evangelists, pastors, and teachers to
the church?

2. Who is it who does "the work of ministry"? Who is supposed to build up the
body of Christ (v. 12)?

3. How should verses 11 and 12 impact what we expect our pastors to do?

4. According to Paul, what is the goal of building up the body of Christ
(vv. 13–14)? What are the different ways Paul describes this goal?

5. What threat to the church's maturity does Paul warn against in verse 14?

6. Paul's picture of a spiritual children being tossed to and fro by bad doctrine
and human cunning is a graphic one. Ironically, the difference between real children and spiritual children is that spiritual children don't always recognize their
immaturity. Building off of what Paul says in verse 14, what would be some concrete signs of spiritual immaturity in someone's life?

7. By what means does Paul exhort the church in Ephesus to combat this threat
of false teaching (vv. 15–16)?

8. What are some concrete ways that you can help others grow in their knowledge of Christ and in resisting winds of doctrine and human schemes?

9. From whom does the body of Christ grow (vv. 15–16)?

10. How does the body of Christ grow? (v. 16)

11. What does this whole passage teach us about the nature of Christian growth?

12. How does this passage confront the person who thinks of himself as a Lone-
Ranger Christian?

13. How should a commitment to build up the body of Christ by speaking the truth in love impact:

    a) Our understanding of "ministry"?
    b) Our finances?
    c) How we use our time?
    d) What we do on Sunday mornings? Sunday afternoons? Other weeknights?

WEEK 6
THE DISTINCT CHURCH

GETTING STARTED

Some church leaders speak as if the church needs to do its best to look and act like the world in order for it to be successful.

Of course such leaders don't want the church to *morally* emulate the world, but they do want the church's music, leadership structures, physical appearance, and way of speaking to make non-Christians feel at home, to feel as if they belong.

It's true, the Bible does call Christians to adapt to others' cultural preferences in order to avoid putting any unnecessary offense in the way of the gospel (1 Cor. 9:19–23). But the impulse to try to make non-Christians feel as comfortable as possible within the church can be a dangerous one. It can lead us to downplay the ways in which the church is meant to be *distinct* from the world.

1. What are some ways in which you think the church should be distinct from the world?

MAIN IDEA

God calls the church to be distinct from the world through our faith in the gospel and conformity to his character.

DIGGING IN

In Matthew 5:13–16 Jesus tells his disciples,

> [13] You are the salt of the earth, but if salt has lost its taste, how shall its saltiness be restored? It is no longer good for anything except to be thrown out and trampled under people's feet.
>
> [14] You are the light of the world. A city set on a hill cannot be hidden. [15] Nor do people light a lamp and put it under a basket, but

on a stand, and it gives light to all in the house. [16] In the same way, let your light shine before others, so that they may see your good works and give glory to your Father who is in heaven.

The common theme in the images of salt and light is that Jesus's disciples are to be distinct from the world and so be a blessing to the world. Salt preserves and gives flavor because of its distinct saltiness. It has to retain that distinct quality, or else it isn't good for anything. Likewise, light shines brightly, illuminating people's way because it stands out from the surrounding darkness.

How are we to be distinct? Consider what Jesus says in the verses just before his words about salt and light:

[3] Blessed are the poor in spirit, for theirs is the kingdom of heaven.
[4] Blessed are those who mourn, for they shall be comforted.
[5] Blessed are the meek, for they shall inherit the earth.
[6] Blessed are those who hunger and thirst for righteousness, for they shall be satisfied.
[7] Blessed are the merciful, for they shall receive mercy.
[8] Blessed are the pure in heart, for they shall see God.
[9] Blessed are the peacemakers, for they shall be called sons of God.
[10] Blessed are those who are persecuted for righteousness' sake, for theirs is the kingdom of heaven.
[11] Blessed are you when others revile you and persecute you and utter all kinds of evil against you falsely on my account. [12] Rejoice and be glad, for your reward is great in heaven, for so they persecuted the prophets who were before you. (Matt. 5:3–12)

1. *What do being poor in spirit, mourning, being meek, and hungering and thirsting after righteousness all have in common (vv. 3–6)?*

2. *What do being merciful, being pure in heart, and being peacemakers all have in common (vv. 7–9)?*

3. *Why do you think people who live and act in these ways would find themselves being persecuted (vv. 10–11)?*

The distinctness Jesus wants his people to have is a distinctness of both broken-hearted trust and faith-fueled obedience. He wants us to be meek and merciful, to be poor in spirit and peacemakers. Our distinctness from the world begins with the recognition that apart from Christ we are utterly lost, utterly sinful, utterly broken. Our distinctness from the world begins, in other words, with repenting of sin and trusting in Christ alone to save us.

Yet while Jesus calls his followers to be salt and light in the world, we don't always live up to that, do we?

Throughout the book of 1 Corinthians, Paul brings the gospel to bear on ways in which the Corinthians were acting more like worldly people than like followers of Christ. In the first four chapters Paul focuses on their wrong attitudes toward Christian leaders, which were resulting in factions and divisions within the church.

Then in chapter 5, Paul addresses a grave moral failure on the part of the whole church. He writes,

> [1] It is actually reported that there is sexual immorality among you, and of a kind that is not tolerated even among pagans, for a man has his father's wife. [2] And you are arrogant! Ought you not rather to mourn? Let him who has done this be removed from among you.
>
> [3] For though absent in body, I am present in spirit; and as if present, I have already pronounced judgment on the one who did such a thing. [4] When you are assembled in the name of the Lord Jesus and my spirit is present, with the power of our Lord Jesus, [5] you are to deliver this man to Satan for the destruction of the flesh, so that his spirit may be saved in the day of the Lord.
>
> [6] Your boasting is not good. Do you not know that a little leaven leavens the whole lump? [7] Cleanse out the old leaven that you may be a new lump, as you really are unleavened. For Christ, our Passover lamb, has been sacrificed. [8] Let us therefore celebrate the festival, not with the old leaven, the leaven of malice and evil, but with the unleavened bread of sincerity and truth.
>
> [9] I wrote to you in my letter not to associate with sexually immoral people— [10] not at all meaning the sexually immoral of this world, or the greedy and swindlers, or idolaters, since then you would need to go out of the world. [11] But now I am writing to you not to associate with anyone who bears the name of brother if he is guilty of sexual immorality or greed, or is an idolater, reviler, drunk-

ard, or swindler—not even to eat with such a one. [12] For what have I
to do with judging outsiders? Is it not those inside the church whom
you are to judge? [13] God judges those outside. "Purge the evil person
from among you." (1 Cor. 5:1–13)

In another volume in this series called *Guarding One Another*, we
explore in greater depth Paul's instruction to put this sinning man
out of the church.

In this study, we will focus on what this passage, especially the
last five verses, calls the church *to be*: a people distinct from the
world.

4. Read verses 9–10. What did Paul tell the Corinthians to do in a former letter?

5. Did Paul mean that the Corinthians should have nothing to do with non-Christians who live this way?

6. What specific instructions does Paul give the Corinthians in verses 11 through 13?

7. In verse 11, Paul emphatically states, "But now I am writing to you not to associate with anyone who bears the name of brother if he is guilty of sexual immorality or greed, or is an idolater, reviler, drunkard, or swindler—not even to eat with such a one."

Why do you think Paul gives opposite instructions regarding how the Corinthians are to treat an immoral person who does not claim to be a Christian and one who does?

8. Read verses 1–2. Who does Paul hold accountable for maintaining the purity of the church?

9. What does this say about your responsibility to the church you're a member of?

10. According to verse 2, the Corinthians not only tolerated this man's immorality, they were puffed up with pride because of their "tolerance"! That's why Paul rebukes the whole church for giving their approval to such behavior.

But this kind of overt boasting is not the only way that a church gives their approval to someone's behavior. Rather, church membership itself is the church's endorsement, as it were, that a person is a Christian. So a church doesn't have to boast about a member's immoral behavior in order to endorse it; simply allowing a person to remain a member of the church is endorsement enough.

What message does it send to the world if a church approves of radically immoral behavior, such as sexual immorality, greed, idolatry, drunkenness, or swindling (see v. 11)?

11. On the other hand, what message does it send to the world when the church's life together is marked by love, unity, forgiveness, and holiness (see John 13:34–35; 17:20–21)?

Not Perfection, but Repentance

Paul's exhortation not to associate with any professing believer who practices the behaviors he lists in verse 11 does *not* mean that a church should consist of only perfect people. Just the opposite! Remember that Jesus says that we are to be spiritually poor, to mourn, and to be meek. All of this implies the ongoing presence of sin in our lives. And it reminds us that we're saved by Christ's work, not our own.

Paul's teaching in this passage is not that the church should exclude imperfect people but people whose sin is so severe and unrepentant that the sin undermines their claim to be a Christian in the first place.

The goal is for the church to be distinct from the world. It should shine with God's holy and righteous character, thereby giving witness to the gospel we preach.

12. What are some ways that you can personally contribute to the church's distinctness, to its task of reflecting God's character to the world?

WEEK 7
THE GOD-GLORIFYING
CHURCH

GETTING STARTED

1. In Matthew 16:18 Jesus says that he will build his church and that the gates of hell will not prevail against it. Why do you think Jesus established a church *instead of a bunch of unassociated individuals?*

MAIN IDEA

God calls the church to display his glory to the world by reflecting his character. The church is central in God's saving purposes because it is the place where he causes his name to be made known and his glory to be put on display.

DIGGING IN

We can begin to answer the question of why Jesus established a church by going back to the Old Testament and considering why God promised to save his people.

In Ezekiel 36:26–27 God promises,

> ²⁶ I will give you a new heart, and a new spirit I will put within you. And I will remove the heart of stone from your flesh and give you a heart of flesh. ²⁷ And I will put my Spirit within you, and cause you to walk in my statutes and be careful to obey my rules.

This is the promise of the new covenant, which Jesus said he would fulfill through his death (Luke 22:20; see also Jer. 31:31–34). But notice what God says in Ezekiel immediately before this promise of a new, decisive, saving work:

^{22} Therefore say to the house of Israel, Thus says the Lord GOD: It is not for your sake, O house of Israel, that I am about to act, but for the sake of my holy name, which you have profaned among the nations to which you came. ^{23} And I will vindicate the holiness of my great name, which has been profaned among the nations, and which you have profaned among them. And the nations will know that I am the LORD, declares the Lord GOD, when through you I vindicate my holiness before their eyes. (36:22–23)

We hear the exact same message about why God saves his people in Isaiah 48:9–11:

^{9} For my name's sake I defer my anger,
   for the sake of my praise I restrain it for you,
   that I may not cut you off.
^{10} Behold, I have refined you, but not as silver;
   I have tried you in the furnace of affliction.
^{11} For my own sake, for my own sake, I do it,
   for how should my name be profaned?
   My glory I will not give to another.

1. Based on these last two passages, how would you summarize God's motivation for acting on behalf of his people, his purpose in saving them?

2. Does this mean that God doesn't save us because he loves us? And does this mean that God is egotistical?

In the rest of this study, we're going to look very briefly at three New Testament passages that all say the same thing from a different angle about why Jesus established a church. Specifically, the three passages we'll consider give us three specific reasons why Jesus established a church.

Reason 1: To Display God's Wisdom

In the New Testament, we see that God's purpose to display his glory comes to fruition through the church. As Paul writes in Ephesians 3:10–11 (NIV),

¹⁰ His intent was that now, through the church, the manifold wisdom of God should be made known to the rulers and authorities in the heavenly realms, ¹¹ according to his eternal purpose that he accomplished in Christ Jesus our Lord.

It is through *the church*, Paul says, that God is now displaying his abundant wisdom to the rulers and authorities in the heavenly places. He is displaying his glory before all the universe through the people he has reconciled to himself in Christ!

3. What is it about the church that enables it to display the wisdom of God? (Hint: You'll find the answer Paul specifically has in mind back in Eph. 2:11–16 and 3:4–6.)

Reason 2: To Display God's Love

In John 13, Jesus washes his disciples' feet as an example of humble service and love and instructs them to follow his example (vv. 14–15). Then, in verses 34 and 35 he tells them:

> ³⁴ A new commandment I give to you, that you love one another: just as I have loved you, you also are to love one another. ³⁵ By this all people will know that you are my disciples, if you have love for one another.

4. What commandment does Jesus give to his disciples in this passage?

5. According to Jesus, what will happen when his disciples obey this command?

6. How does our love for one another display God's glory?

Reason 3: To Display God's Oneness

In John 17:20–23, Jesus prays:

> ²⁰ I do not ask for these only, but also for those who will believe in me through their word, ²¹ that they may all be one, just as you, Father, are in me, and I in you, that they also may be in us, so that the world may believe that you have sent me. ²² The glory that you have given

me I have given to them, that they may be one even as we are one, 23 I in them and you in me, that they may become perfectly one, so that the world may know that you sent me and loved them even as you loved me.

7. What does Jesus pray for his disciples in this passage?

8. What result does Jesus see happening when God answers his prayer for his disciples' unity (see vv. 21, 23)?

It is in the local church that the love and unity Jesus prays his disciples would have comes to its fullest and most concrete expression. When Christians commit to love one another, to bear one another's burdens, to submit to one another, to encourage and instruct one another, and to preserve the unity of faith together— which is what church membership *is*—they display God's glory in their life together.

9. How does the unity of a local church display God's glory?

10. What are common reasons people go to church? According to the passages we've studied today, why should we want to go to church?

It's in the local church that the wisdom, love, and oneness of God are most concretely and visibly displayed as people who are very different in the world's eyes worship God together, serve each other, and build each other up in the knowledge of Christ.

That is why the local church is such a crucial aspect of God's plan of salvation: it's where God intends to display his glory to the watching world.

TEACHER'S NOTES FOR WEEK 1

DIGGING IN

1. Paul teaches that we were "far off" (v. 17), and were "strangers and aliens" (v. 19). Both images communicate that in our lost state we were not only alienated from God, but also were separated and excluded from God's people.

2. In verse 19 Paul teaches that we are now "fellow citizens with the saints," and members of God's household. These phrases indicate that when we became Christians, we were not only reconciled to God but also brought into the fellowship of his people.

3. As Christians, we should *not* view ourselves as autonomous individuals. Rather, we should view ourselves as fellow citizens of God's people and members of God's household. While we still retain our individual identity and responsibilities, we also take on the new identity and responsibilities that belong to the people of God. For instance, Paul says we "are being built together into a dwelling place for God by the Spirit." That means God's Spirit dwells among us specially through our togetherness. There are things we are together that we are not apart.

4. Second Corinthians 6 teaches that Christians are:

- The temple of God (v. 16)
- God's people (v. 16)
- God's children (v. 18)

5. The term "people of God" signifies that Christians are possessed by God and that the world will identify us with him. His name is on us, and what we do will make the world think one way or another about him.

In light of this, we are obligated to separate from what is unholy. More broadly, we are obligated to obey God, to pursue holiness, and to reflect God's character to the world. See, for example, Exodus 19:5–6, where God tells Israel that he redeemed them from Egypt so that they would become a "kingdom of priests and a holy nation." They were to show the world what he is like.

6. The people of God are to represent *God's* character. This contradicts and overturns our desire to be autonomous ("a law unto ourselves") because it means that we are called to submit to God's will in all things.

7. Possible answers for question (a): we're no longer autonomous but are to commit ourselves to other Christians by joining a local church and living faithfully in that church; we're to bear one another's burdens and rejoice with one another (see Rom. 12:15; 1 Cor. 12:26; Gal. 6:21); we're to seek not our own good but the common good because we recognize that, as a people, we belong to one another.

Possible answers for the question (b) include: we would recognize that we are to witness to non-Christians by being distinct from them; while we should love and care for non-Christians, we should not partner with them in any ways that compromise the gospel.

8. Possible answers include: we would be more diligent to pursue unity; we would strive together for holiness; we would bear with one another patiently.

9. Answers will vary.

10. Answers will vary, but they should reflect that, since Alyssa is a member of God's people, she has a special obligation to obey God in every area of life. This includes breaking off this relationship with a non-Christian (see, for example, 2 Cor. 6:14). Therefore, in appropriate ways, both individual church members and, if necessary, church leaders, should be involved in helping Alyssa to obey God in this area of her life. In other words, what Alyssa does with her so-called "private" life *is* the church's business, because Alyssa is a member of the people of God. Our lives reflect on one another, and all of us are called to reflect God's holy character every area of our lives.

TEACHER'S NOTES FOR WEEK 2

DIGGING IN

1. The overarching metaphor Paul uses in this chapter is a body and its members.

2. In verses 15 and 16, the foot and the ear say, "Because I am not a _____ (hand/eye), I am not a part of the body." This expresses a feeling of inferiority, of not being needed, and of feeling excluded from the body.

3. Paul responds with two main points: (1) it is the very nature of a body to have many members; if a body *didn't* have many different members it wouldn't be a body (vv. 17, 19–20); and (2) God is the one who has sovereignly determined how the members would be arranged (v. 18).

4. People who are tempted to think like the "foot" and the "ear" should recognize that they are integral parts of the body. Their unique gifts are important for the body's well-being. Therefore, they should not feel excluded from the body or attempt to cut themselves off from it. Rather, they should participate in building up the body.

5. In verse 21 the "eye" and the "head" say, "I have no need of you" to the other members of the body. This expresses self-sufficiency, independence, and arrogance.

6. There are two main points in Paul's response: (1) we treat the less honorable and presentable parts of our physical bodies with special honor, which means we should treat the "less honorable" members of the church with special honor (vv. 22–24a); and (2) God has deliberately arranged the body this way, giving honor to the parts that lacked it, in order that the body would be unified and that the various parts would care for one another (vv. 24b–25).

7. In verse 22, Paul says that the parts of the body that seem to be weaker are indispensable. This means that we should regard church members who do not seem impressive as essential to the health of the body, so we should give them special honor and care. We must recognize that the body will only grow as it should when each member functions properly (Eph. 4:16), including those members whom we are tempted to scorn or disregard.

8. In this verse, God has two goals for arranging the body as he has: (1) so that there would be no division in the body; and (2) so that the members would have the same care for one another. Verse 26 illustrates this by

observing that if any member suffers, the other members suffer together with it, and if any member is honored, all the other members rejoice with it.

9. There are a range of appropriate answers to this question. For example, a Lone-Ranger Christian is mistaken because *he* needs the body in order to be built up, challenged, and kept accountable (see Heb. 3:12; 10:24–25). He's also mistaken because *the body* needs him in order to function properly. In other words, being concerned with his own personal relationship with God means helping other Christians grow and persevere in faith.

10–11. Answers will vary.

TEACHER'S NOTES FOR WEEK 3

DIGGING IN

1. The images and metaphors Paul uses to describe Jews' and Gentiles' new unity in Christ are:

- Fellow citizens
- Members of God's household
- Building/temple

2. In verse 20, Paul writes that the church is built on the foundation of the apostles and prophets. This refers to the authoritative, Spirit-inspired foundation of teaching that the apostles and the authors of the Old Testament provided for the church. Today, we possess the apostles' authoritative teaching in the New Testament. This foundation is essential for the life and health of the church because the gospel is what saves us and creates the church, and the Bible is the food that nurtures Christian growth.

3. No, a Christian is not living in light of this truth if he or she is not a member of a church. He is more like a lone brick lying on the ground than a stone fitted and joined into a temple.

4. One could encourage such a Christian by reminding him or her that our very identity in Christ (as a stone in the temple) means that we are meant to be solidly committed to, built into, and joined to the other stones in the temple. One could also encourage such a person to join a church based on the church's mandate to be holy, which requires Christians to hold one another accountable and submit to one another. This can't be done when a person maintains his or her autonomy and the right to leave at any time without consequence!

5. The church's numerical growth takes place as people hear the gospel, believe it, and are saved (Acts 2:41). The church's spiritual growth occurs through the Word of God, as believers speak the truth to one another in love (Eph. 4:15–16).

6. The Holy Spirit builds the temple that is the church.

7. The Holy Spirit builds this temple *in* Christ.

8. The Holy Spirit builds this temple as a dwelling place *for* God the Father.

9. This should encourage Christians for several reasons:

- It reminds us that, because we are "in Christ," we have been reconciled to God and thus receive "every spiritual blessing" (Eph. 1:3).
- It reminds us that building the church is ultimately the Spirit's work.
- It points us toward God's ultimate purpose and promise to one day dwell with his people in perfect fellowship (Rev. 21:3–4).

10. The fact that the church *is* a holy temple means that:

a) The church should interview prospective members in order to learn their testimonies, attempt to discern whether they understand and believe the gospel, and ensure (to the best of human ability) that there is no obvious contradiction between their profession of faith and how they live.

b) The church *should* actively seek to oversee its members' lives. The church should do this in order to encourage them and hold them accountable to live, by God's grace, in a manner worthy of their calling to be God's holy people.

c) The church should obey Jesus by excluding from church membership any professing Christian who does not repent of sin (see Matt. 18:15–20).

11. Answers will vary, but the basic idea in all of these is that we should seek to participate in the life of the church in such a way that we will grow in holiness and help other church members do the same.

TEACHER'S NOTES FOR WEEK 4

DIGGING IN

1. This new covenant differs from the old in that:

- The law will be written on the people's hearts, enabling them to keep it (v. 33).
- All of God's people will know the Lord personally (v. 34).
- God will forgive their sins decisively and finally (v. 34).

2. Given the realities of the new covenant,

   a) Someone cannot be a Christian yet never grow spiritually. To be a member of the new covenant is to have God's law written on your heart and his Spirit within you (see Ezek. 36:27), enabling you to live an increasingly holy life.
   b) Yet this does *not* mean that every day of our lives will be marked by bold and dramatic growth. Some days, weeks, and months will be better than others. But spiritual growth should be the general trend of our lives over the course of years.

3. These passages convey the expectation that every member of the church will grow spiritually and will contribute to the growth of the entire church body. Peter expects that every believer will offer up "spiritual sacrifices" that are acceptable to God, and Paul says that the body grows through the contribution of every single member.

4. This growth doesn't happen all by ourselves. Rather, Christians grow *together* as every member contributes to the body's growth.

5. When Paul preached the gospel to the Thessalonians, they received it in the midst of much affliction, but they still responded with joy (v. 6). That is, they joyfully embraced the gospel even though it led to being persecuted for their faith. Further, they turned from idols to serve the living and true God (v. 9).

6. A true Christian begins a new life of trusting in Christ, turning from sin and obeying God from the heart. A nominal Christian may give the appearance of those things, but his or her heart has not truly been changed.

Over time, that lack of a changed heart will show itself in a failure to grow spiritually.

7. Paul attributes their responses to the power of the Holy Spirit (vv. 5–6). This leaves no room for boasting because our salvation is entirely by God's grace and through his power.

8. The fact that the Thessalonians received the gospel in much affliction testifies to the genuineness of their faith because it shows that they were willing to suffer for Christ's sake as soon as they received the gospel. When confronted with immediate suffering for the sake of Christ, they chose to believe and to suffer rather than to be comfortable by rejecting Christ. Thus, the price they paid to be Christians testifies that their faith was genuine.

9. The Thessalonians' faith prompted them:

- To works of faith and labors of love (v. 3)
- To proclaim the gospel (v. 8a)
- To serve the true God (v. 9)
- To wait for the return of Christ (v. 10)

10. If you do perceive a lack of joy, a lack of conviction, and a lack of turning from idols in your life, then the solution is to trust in Christ, to cling to him by faith. Rather than despair, turn to Christ in faith because he is a Savior for sinners.

11–12. Answers will vary.

TEACHER'S NOTES FOR WEEK 5

DIGGING IN

1. Christ gave apostles, prophets, evangelists, pastors, and teachers to the church to equip the saints for the work of ministry, so that all the saints would be able to build up the body of Christ (v. 12). Christ gave these as gifts to the church so that they would teach, train, and equip the church in order that *every member* would be able to contribute to the body's growth.

2. All the saints do the work of ministry (v. 12). Every member of the church is to build up the body.

3. Here are two ways verses 11 and 12 should impact our expectations for our pastors:

- First, in light of these verses, we should expect our pastors to devote themselves to teaching the Word and training and equipping the saints for service.
- Second, this means that we should *not* expect them to do all the ministry *for* the church, but to equip the body to build itself up in love.

4. According to Paul, the goal of building up the body is that the whole body would be mature in Christ. Paul describes this maturity in terms of unity in belief (v. 13), attaining to the full measure of Christ's maturity (v. 13), and being doctrinally sound and stable in order to resist false teaching (v. 14).

5. In verse 14 Paul warns against false teaching as a threat to the church's health. Note that such false teaching is not always obvious: it seeks to subvert the church through "craftiness" and "deceitful schemes," which means that we must always be on guard against it.

6. There are a number of signs of immaturity: getting easily caught up in new ideas, books, or teachings; getting quickly excited by charismatic personalities; drawing drastic conclusions with the onset of difficulties; being easily influenced by others; tending to believe emotions more than truth; becoming quickly discouraged when emotions don't always keep up with truth; and so on.

7. Paul exhorts the Ephesians to counter the threat of false teaching by "speaking the truth in love" (v. 15). This means that every Christian is to

resist false doctrine and promote sound doctrine by speaking the truth to others. Thus, in some sense, *every* Christian is to teach the Bible to others.

8. Answers will vary.

9. The body's growth is *from Christ*.

10. The body of Christ grows:

- As we speak the truth in love to one another (v. 15)
- As every joint holds the body together (v. 16; this may be a reference to the special role that pastors and teachers play in equipping the body)
- As *each part*—that is, every single member of the church!—works properly (v. 16)

11. This passage teaches a number of things about Christian growth.

- The task of pastors and teachers is to equip Christians to help *them* help others grow (vv. 11–12).
- Christian growth means growth in the knowledge of Christ (vv. 13–14).
- Speaking the truth in love is the means by which we are to help others grow (vv. 15–16).
- Christian growth is thoroughly corporate: every member of the body contributes to the church's growth, which means that every member of the body should be helping others grow and be helped by others to grow.
- Christian growth—specifically the growth of the church as a corporate whole—is *from Christ* (v. 16).

12. This passage confronts the Lone-Ranger Christian by exploding the idea that one can grow best as a Christian by oneself. This passage teaches that we all grow in Christ as members of a body, as each member of that body contributes. The Lone-Ranger Christian is not only missing out on how God wants *him or her* to grow but is also disobeying God's call to build up others in the church through committed, accountable relationships.

13. A commitment to build up the body of Christ should have these implications (among others):

- a) We should understand ministry to be something that every church member is called to do, not merely pastors!
- b) We should give joyfully to our own local church's work of bringing

saints to maturity in Christ, and we should view all of our finances as a stewardship from God to use not only to provide for ourselves but also to further the work of the gospel.

c) Very practically, we should work deliberate times of spiritual conversation, prayer, and Bible study *with other Christians* into our schedules in order to build up the body of Christ by speaking the truth in love.

d) On Sunday mornings, first of all, we should regularly assemble with God's people. Second, we should approach the church's gatherings as an opportunity to worship God, to be built up in faith, *and* to serve others and build them up in the knowledge of Christ. Practically, this means approaching church with an eye toward serving others. Can you help out with what needs to be done? Can you greet the people who look like visitors, get to know them, maybe introduce them to someone with whom they would connect well? Can you get to know the church member who seems stuck on the fringes of church life? Can you approach someone after the sermon with an encouraging reflection from that morning's Scripture passage? These kinds of activities should carry into the afternoon and, indeed, all week.

TEACHER'S NOTES FOR WEEK 6

DIGGING IN

1. All these things reflect our sinfulness, spiritual poverty, and need for a Savior. Unlike the world, which glories in pride and self-sufficiency, Jesus's followers recognize that we are totally dependent on him to save us. Thus:

- We should be poor in spirit, recognizing our sinfulness.
- We should mourn over our sin and its effects.
- We should be meek, recognizing how far short of God's glory we fall.
- We should hunger and thirst for righteousness, recognizing that we lack it in ourselves but that Christ is able to supply what we lack.

2. All these are virtues and actions that reflect the character of God. God is merciful toward us. God is utterly pure. God is the great peacemaker, who sent Christ into the world to reconcile his enemies to himself. Thus, these are all ways in which those who follow Christ will positively reflect God's character.

3. Answers will vary. One reason why people who act in these ways will be persecuted is that sin loves the darkness and hates to be exposed (John 3:20). When people mourn their sin, are poor in spirit, and live in a way that reflects God's character, it exposes others' sin, which in turn provokes their defensive hostility.

4. In a former letter, Paul told the Corinthians not to associate with any sexually immoral people, by whom he meant any professing Christians who were sexually immoral (or immoral in the other ways he mentions in verse 10).

5. Paul did *not* mean that the Corinthians were to disassociate themselves from any non-Christians who behaved in these ways, but only from professing Christians who did.

6. In verse 11 Paul reiterates his former instructions to the Corinthians, namely, that they should not associate or even eat with a professing Christian whose life is marked by seriously immoral behavior. In verse 12 he explains that the Corinthians are to judge those who are inside the

church. This doesn't mean that they are to be vindictive or legalistic or think that their judgment is the last word about a person. It *does* mean that they are to hold members of their church accountable to live as Christians. As verse 13 specifies, this means that the Corinthians should exclude from the church's membership any person who professes faith in Christ but lives in a radically immoral way.

7. Paul gives opposite instructions about how the Corinthians are to interact with immoral non-Christians and immoral professing Christians because he only expects Christians to live like Christians!

It's also clear that Paul is concerned about the church's corporate testimony before the world. It is the person who "bears the name of brother" who is to be excluded from the church if he persists in serious immorality. Paul exhorts the church to separate from such people because if we don't, we give the impression that this way of living is consistent with being a Christian. If we Christians live like non-Christians, our actions lie about who Jesus is and what he came to do.

8. Paul holds the Corinthian church as a whole accountable for the purity of the church. In some sense, every member of the church is at fault when the church tolerates, and thereby gives approval to, immorality.

9. Paul holding the entire church accountable means that you are responsible to uphold sound teaching. You are to pursue holiness. And you are to spiritually engage others in such a way that you can encourage them in holiness and rebuke sin in their lives.

10. When a church tolerates serious immorality it sends a series of lying messages to the world:

- That this way of living is consistent with being a Christian
- That those who live this way may inherit the kingdom of heaven (see Paul's explicit statement to the contrary in 1 Corinthians 6:9–11)
- That the gospel is not really powerful to transform sinners
- That God isn't really concerned that we live holy lives, and so on

11. When the church's life is marked by love, unity, forgiveness, and holiness, it sends the world the message that:

- Christ *is* powerful to transform sin
- God is holy, demands holiness, and empowers his people to live holy lives

- There is a radical distinction between those who belong to Christ and those who do not, and so on

12. Answers will vary.

TEACHER'S NOTES FOR WEEK 7

DIGGING IN

1. God's motivation for and purpose in saving his people is to display his glory.

2. The fact that God saves us in order to display his glory does not rule out the fact that God saves us because he loves us (John 3:16). God saves us for his own reasons, not because of anything good we've done, but in order to make known the riches of his mercy upon people who don't deserve it (see Romans 9). In other words, God's highest purpose in saving us—his chief motivation—is his own glory. Does this mean that God is egotistical? Certainly not! While it would be wrong for any human to act for the sake of his own glory, it is absolutely right for God to act for his own glory, because God is infinitely perfect and glorious. Who else's glory should be our chief end?

3. According to Paul, the reconciliation of Jew and Gentile manifests God's wisdom because it is in the church—the local church—that these two groups of people who were formerly separated and hostile toward each other now unite in one body. Today, we could apply this more broadly to the members of the church generally. The church consists of people who have nothing in common but Christ, and who now treat each other as brothers and sisters. This unity is expressed in the church in concrete, practical ways as these former enemies love each other, serve each other, and bear each other's burdens. Thus, God's wisdom is put on display in that he is able to make enemies into brothers, which is practically displayed through the life of the church.

4. In this passage Jesus commands his disciples to love one another as he has loved them (v. 34).

5. When Jesus's disciples obey this command, all people will know that they are his disciples (v. 35).

6. Our love for one another displays God's glory in that our actions display God's own character. Our love for one another also displays God's glory in that it shows that God's grace is powerful to transform us selfish sinners into people who willingly lay down our lives for one another.

7. In this passage Jesus prays that his disciples would be one, just as he and the Father are one (see vv. 21, 23).

8. The result of the disciples' unity is that the world will believe that God sent him and will know that God has loved Jesus's disciples even as he has loved Jesus (vv. 21, 23). That is, the disciples' love for one another will show the world something of who Jesus is and will testify to his divine mission.

9. Christian unity displays God's glory in that we provide a picture of the unity that exists between Father, Son, and Holy Spirit. According to Jesus's prayer, Christian unity is in some sense a display of God's own unity. Christian unity also displays God's glory because it demonstrates that the gospel powerfully overcomes all kinds of barriers that typically divide people.

10. Answers will vary.

9Marks

Building Healthy Churches

9Marks exists to equip church leaders with a biblical vision and practical resources for displaying God's glory to the nations through healthy churches.

To that end, we want to see churches characterized by these nine marks of health:

1 Expositional Preaching
2 Biblical Theology
3 A Biblical Understanding of the Gospel
4 A Biblical Understanding of Conversion
5 A Biblical Understanding of Evangelism
6 Biblical Church Membership
7 Biblical Church Discipline
8 Biblical Discipleship
9 Biblical Church Leadership

Find all our Crossway titles
and other resources at
www.9Marks.org

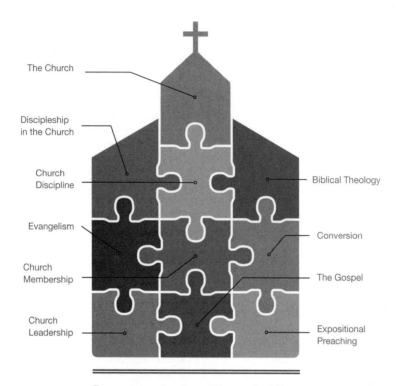

The Church

Discipleship in the Church

Church Discipline

Evangelism

Church Membership

Church Leadership

Biblical Theology

Conversion

The Gospel

Expositional Preaching

Be sure to check out the rest of the
9MARKS HEALTHY CHURCH STUDY GUIDE SERIES

This series covers the nine distinctives of a healthy church as originally laid out in *Nine Marks of a Healthy Church* by Mark Dever. Each book explores the biblical foundations of key aspects of the church, helping Christians to live out those realities as members of a local body. A perfect resource for use in Sunday school, church-wide studies, or small group contexts.